An Amazing Life

THE EXTRAORDINARY LIFE OF A FRIEND OF
GOD AND HOW TO BECOME ONE

BOLA OLIVIA OGEDENGBE

AN AMAZING LIFE
Copyright © 2020 Bola Olivia Ogedengbe
All rights reserved.

No part of this publication may be reproduced, stored in a retrieval system, distributed, or transmitted in any form or by any means, including photocopying, recording, or other electronic or mechanical methods, except for brief quotations in printed reviews, without the prior written permission of the publisher.

All Scripture quotations, unless otherwise indicated, are taken from the New International Version. Used by permission.
Printed in France

ISBN: 9791095039297

First published: January 2020

OTHER BOOKS BY AUTHOR
Reborn, A New Identity
Reborn, 30 day devotional/Workbook
An Eye to the Crown
Appelez à l'Existence (Cell into Existence)
Le Feu de Dieu (the Fire of God)
An Amazing Life

Dedication

I wish to honour my leaders and mentors who have shown me the way in ministry and life. They taught and are still teaching me to walk in faith, honour God and live a life of excellence.

TABLE OF CONTENTS

Introduction to divine friendship *1*

BOOK ONE - BENEFITS OF BEING A FRIEND OF GOD *11*

Access to divine secrets 13

Divine Interaction 23

Favour and influence with God 33

The faithfulness of God - Divine Intervention 43

BOOK TWO - BECOMING A FRIEND OF GOD *53*

Know Him 55

Trust Him 65

Agree with Him 75

Obey Him 85

Commune with Him 95

Honour Him 105

Epilogue 115

About the Author 117

Other books by author 119

INTRODUCTION TO DIVINE FRIENDSHIP

TRUE FRIENDSHIP IS ONE OF THE SWEETEST things on the face of the earth and is very beneficial for both parties. Relationship with God is enjoyable; it is profitable, not an inconvenience imposed on mankind in exchange for escaping hell. It is not a relationship between equals and does not altogether parallel human friendships. So it is very striking that God calls Abraham 'my friend'. And I cannot but wonder, 'what did God like about Abraham'?

Truth be told, divine friendship is offered to us for our good and must be the quest of every believer. However, we live in a fallen world where the things of God can be alien to us. So we must cry out to God for a heart that wants the right things, a heart that craves intimacy with God, and friendship with God.

To spur you on to holy desire, consider the impact Abraham's friendship with God had on his life. Every good thing God desires from us is the outcome of some other good thing He had previously given to us. God showed Abraham great kindness and treated him marvellously. Abraham, though imperfect, reciprocated in faith and obedience, and as he matured in faith, conducted himself in a way that honoured God. We will study what in his attitude towards God qualified him to be called a friend of God. May the brilliance of this friendship stir you up to greater expectation in your friendship with God.

Scripture

Read John 15. Write a summary of the chapter and emphasise the particular points relevant to this topic.

Questions

Read the Introduction from the book to answer the following questions.

1. How would you define friendship?

2. Who is a friend of God?

3. Explain God's initial plan of friendship with mankind.

4. Give examples of individuals in the Old Testament who surpassed their contemporaries in developing a strong relationship with God.

5. What did they do that you can emulate?

INSIGHT

A VERY SPECIAL RELATIONSHIP

Israel was very conscious of their special relationship with God that began with Abraham. James testifies that Abraham believed God, and he was called God's friend. He was one man who obeyed God and forever set the course for his descendants and for the entire world.

That is why when David stood before Goliath, he fearlessly declared his stand as one who had a covenant with God. That is why when Jehoshaphat had to face the armies of the Ammonites and Moabites, hellbent on destroying Judah, he invoked the friendship of God and Abraham.

He called the people to fasting and prayer. They came from every town in Judah, gathered before the Lord's temple and Jehoshaphat cried out to God. Listen to him.

> Lord, the God of our ancestors, are you not the God who is in heaven? You rule over all the kingdoms of the nations. Power and might are in your hand, and no one can withstand you. Did you not, our God, drive out the inhabitants of this land before your people Israel, and give it forever to the descendants of Abraham your friend? (2 Chronicles 20:6).

He reminded God that He Himself had given the land to Israel. He had forbidden Israel, on their way into the Promised Land, from attacking the Ammonites and Moabites. And the Israelites had left them alone. Now the same people were repaying them with evil. But notice he draws God's attention to who Israel was, the 'descendants of Abraham your friend'.

As for their opponents, they were the descendants of Lot who went away from Jehovah to dwell in Sodom. God heard and answered his prayers. The Ammonites and Moabites were soundly defeated and God spared the descendants of His friend Abraham.

6. Why did God call Abraham His friend?

7. What benefits did his descendants derive from the friendship?

8. What does John 15 teach us about friendship with God?

9. Who did Jesus call His friends and why?

10. What is the state of your relationship with God today? Are you a friend of God?

PRAYER

1. Pray for insight into divine friendship.
2. Pray that you will develop a craving to be intimate with God.
3. Pray that God will enlarge your capacity for spiritual things.
4. Pray that every hindrance to your intimacy with God will melt away and disappear.

PROPHETIC DECLARATIONS

1. Declare that you are a friend of God.
2. Declare that you have insight and understanding of the purpose of divine friendship.
3. Declare that all your life you will walk intimately with God.
4. Declare that you will honour the Lord in all things.

YOUR PRAYER/PRAISE POINTS

-
-
-
-
-
-
-

YOUR NOTES

This is where you write everything on your heart that does not fit into any of the other categories.

Your Decisions

Write out at least three things you have decided to do following this study.

BOOK ONE - BENEFITS OF BEING A FRIEND OF GOD

Listen to me, you who pursue righteousness and who seek the Lord: Look to the rock from which you were cut and to the quarry from which you were hewn; look to Abraham, your father, and to Sarah, who gave you birth. When I called him he was only one man, and I blessed him and made him many (Isaiah 51:1-2).

THE PROPHET ISAIAH SPEAKING FOR GOD LEFT the above testimony. When God encountered Abraham, he was a nobody with nothing much going for him. His relationship with God turned his life in the right direction.

God invites us to contemplate his experience knowing that it can be ours. Even as He was faithful to take him from nothing to significance, He will do the same for you if you trust Him.

God took good care of His friend. He wants

you to know that He will do the same for you.

1

Access to divine secrets

As the sun was setting, Abram fell into a deep sleep, and a thick and dreadful darkness came over him. Then the Lord said to him, "Know for certain that for four hundred years your descendants will be strangers in a country not their own and that they will be enslaved and mistreated there. But I will punish the nation they serve as slaves, and afterward they will come out with great possessions. You, however, will go to your ancestors in peace and be buried at a good old age. In the fourth generation your descendants will come back here, for the sin of the Amorites has not yet reached its full measure" (Genesis 15:12-16).

WE WATCH AWED AND JOYFUL AS ISRAEL leaves Egypt and crosses the Red Sea. But rarely do we cast our minds back to the day when God gave this information in advance to Abraham. Some of the people of Israel in slavery in Egypt complained when Moses' efforts to rescue them seemed counterproductive. Many had obviously resigned themselves to perpetual captivity. But Moses succeeded, and they left. They even experienced a splendid deliverance at the Red Sea. But in the wilderness, they grumbled continuously and often sought and plotted to return.

Yet their ancestor, hundreds of years removed from their predicament had clear and accurate information of what the outcome would be. God had given him the information in advance. These, however, knew it second hand only. Insight, knowledge and information can make the difference between success and failure, joy and sorrow, peace and trouble. God alone knows all we need to know. And this is one of the privileges of being a friend of God, having access to divine secrets.

SCRIPTURE

Read Genesis 15. Write a summary of the chapter and emphasise the particular points that are relevant to this topic.

Questions

Read the chapter in the book to answer the following questions.

5. What did God tell Abraham about his descendants? Be specific.

6. Why was this information given to Abraham?

7. In what other instance mentioned in the chapter did God give Abraham information others did not have? What use was this information?

8. What impact did the lack of access to divine secrets have on the life of Lot?

Insight

WE NEED TO SEE

Most people mean well for themselves and their children. Abraham meant well for himself and his nephew. And he was able to do what was best for his nephew because he could get direction from heaven. It is essential that we live intimately with God and hear from Him. Otherwise, we may take decisions that will hinder rather than help the destinies of the precious lives entrusted to our care. That is what Lot did in moving away from Abraham and to the neighbourhood of Sodom.

> "HOW MANY WAYS DO WE HINDER OUR OWN LIVES AND MAKE DECISIONS THAT HARM OUR CHILDREN'S DESTINY BECAUSE WE FAIL TO SEE WHAT GOD IS DOING AND WHAT HE IS SHOWING US?"

9. Comment on the above statement.

_____
_____
_____
_____
_____
_____
_____
_____

10. What specific benefits did Abraham and his family derive from Abraham's access to divine secrets?

___

11. Read John 15:15. What does it say about friendship with God and access to divine secrets?

___

12. The Bible says that "The secret counsel of the Lord is for those who fear Him, and He reveals His covenant to them" (Psalm 25:14). What does that mean and how can you apply it to your life today?

___

13. In the book, I share testimonies of divine secrets being revealed to me about specific steps to take at different times in life and ministry. Have you had a similar experience? List such instances in your life and the impact they made on you.

14. Do you have any such stories of persons who received precious information from God? What difference did it make to their lives?

PRAYER

1. Pray for access to the secret of the Lord.
2. Pray that anything hidden in your life will be made known.
3. Pray that God will increase your spiritual perception.
4. Pray that every hindrance to your capacity to hear God will be removed.

PROPHETIC DECLARATIONS

1. Declare that you are free of blindness and spiritual ignorance.
2. Declare that you have access to the secret of God.
3. Declare that you are attentive to divine direction.
4. Declare that you hear and obey.

YOUR PRAYER/PRAISE POINTS

-
-
-
-
-
-
-
-
-

Your Notes

This is where you write everything on your heart that does not fit into any of the other categories.

YOUR DECISIONS

Write out at least three things you have decided to do following this study.

2

DIVINE INTERACTION

Jesus answered, "If anyone loves Me, he will keep My word. My Father will love him, and We will come to him and make Our home with him. The one who doesn't love Me will not keep My words. The word that you hear is not Mine but is from the Father who sent Me. "I have spoken these things to you while I remain with you. But the Counselor, the Holy Spirit—the Father will send Him in My name—will teach you all things and remind you of everything I have told you" (John 14:23-26 (HCSB)).

WE SAW IN THE PREVIOUS CHAPTER THE captivating exchange between Abraham and God recounted in Genesis 15. It was one of several. A man of idol worshipping stock encounters the one true God and stays in fellowship with Him for the rest of his life. God is still offering intimacy and continuous interaction. The beauty of a man's life is in proportion to his interaction with and revelation of God. It is part of our birthright as New Testament believers. The transcendent God has come to us, to abide with us.

Flaming torches are no longer necessary, nor the voice speaking from heaven. God Himself has come to dwell with us. So, our fellowship and interaction with Him should be even richer and fuller than what Abraham enjoyed. And it is available to all. As with Abraham, the presence of God will be with you. The conversation and the counsel of God will be with you as you draw nearer and nearer to God.

Scripture

Read Acts 7:2-4; John 14:23-26. What are the key points in these passages relevant to this topic?

QUESTIONS

Read the chapter in the book and answer the following questions.

1. Is Abraham a special case? Did he enjoy such interaction with God because he was the father of the faith? Explain.

2. "The beauty of a man's life is in proportion to his interaction with and revelation of God." Comment on this statement.

3. God calls Himself Abraham's shield and great reward. Explain that statement.

4. Discuss two of the interactions between God and Abraham. What happened and what do you learn from them?

5. What impact did the interactions have on Abraham?

INSIGHT

OUR BIRTHRIGHT OF INTIMACY

At Sinai, the presence of God was terrifying. The people drew back fearful, enjoining Moses to speak to God and relate to them whatever He said. But they had no desire for a direct encounter. The privilege of encounter is available for all in Christ Jesus. Yet many still say 'go and talk to God on my behalf and come back and talk to me.' They will not draw near. We too, like Moses, can keep asking for deeper interaction with Him. That is the privilege of friends.

While some prefer for God to remain in His domain while they do their own thing, many are eager for continuous and increasingly deeper interaction with God. Such was the case of Moses. It was the experience of Abraham, and it should be our desire and experience. Even under the Old Covenant, God always wanted His people to be close to Him. Under the New Covenant, the Holy Spirit facilitates interaction with God. The believer is to walk in constant interaction with God as Jesus did with the Father. He heard Him, saw Him, spoke to Him constantly.

6. What difference does the coming of Jesus make in your relationship with God and potential friendship with Him?

7. "... our fellowship and interaction with Him should be even richer and fuller than what Abraham enjoyed." Do you agree or disagree with this quote from the book; in light of the fact that God Himself called Abraham His friend? Explain your position.

_____
_____
_____
_____
_____
_____
_____
_____
_____
_____
_____
_____
_____

8. What is the role of the Holy Spirit in the interaction between men and God?

_____
_____
_____
_____
_____
_____
_____

9. What is your personal experience of interaction with God?

10. Moses cried out to see the glory of God in Exodus 33:18-20. What does that mean? And what do you learn from this encounter?

PRAYER

1. Pray for a greater desire for intimacy with God.

2. Pray that you will be sensitive to the interventions of the Holy Spirit in your life.

3. Pray that you will have the heart to obey every divine instruction and honour every divine encounter.

4. Pray that, like Abraham, the purpose of God will be fully performed in your life.

PROPHETIC DECLARATIONS

1. Declare that you have continuous interaction with the Father.
2. Declare that the Holy Spirit is your Helper and your Friend.
3. Declare that you are directed by the Spirit of God in all things.
4. Declare that you are fully surrendered to God.

YOUR PRAYER/PRAISE POINTS

-
-
-
-
-
-
-
-

Your Notes

This is where you write everything on your heart that does not fit into any of the other categories.

Your Decisions

Write out at least three things you have decided to do following this study.

3

FAVOUR AND INFLUENCE WITH GOD

> So when God destroyed the cities of the plain, he remembered Abraham, and he brought Lot out of the catastrophe that overthrew the cities where Lot had lived (Genesis 19:29).

WHO YOU KNOW DETERMINES WHAT YOU EXPERIENCE. Knowing God sets us apart for a life of fulfilment. And it also makes us a dispenser of good to others. Lot's life was spared along with his two daughters because of his connection to Abraham and Abraham's connection to God. Abraham had previously engaged in intercession for the cities to be judged, but he did not go far enough and could not avert the disaster.

However, when the time for judgement came, God specially dispatched His angel to rescue Lot and his family. The entire city perished. They alone were saved, and all because his uncle had favour with God. We are not even allowed to speculate or suppose that Lot himself might have had something to do with it. No, the Bible clearly states that when the time for destruction came, God remembered Abraham and brought Lot out. He brought him out solely for the sake of Abraham, to spare him grief.

SCRIPTURE

Read Genesis 19. Write out the key lessons from the chapter.

_____
_____
_____
_____
_____
_____
_____
_____
_____
_____
_____
_____

QUESTIONS

Read the chapter in the book and answer the following questions.

1. How would you define favour?

_____
_____
_____

2. Define influence. How does it differ from favour?

3. Give one instance of Abraham enjoying the favour of God though he did not deserve it. Explain why.

4. Had Ishmael not enjoyed favour what would his destiny have been?

5. Why would God show favour to Lot when he had left Abraham and taken the best land?

INSIGHT

INTERCESSION

Abraham pleaded for his son and God said He had heard him. And because of that, he favoured Ishmael. He would not be the chosen son but he would be well taken care of because Abraham had influence with God. Later on, another man who had influence with God obtained favour for a people. In Exodus 32:9–11, Moses pleaded for Israel when God was going to destroy them in His anger at their incessant rebellion. He cried out to God on their behalf. God granted his request and spared Israel.

Intercessory prayer is a powerful act whereby a person who has influence with God asks for favour on behalf of another who is in difficulty. There was one unfortunate instance in God's Word when He sought for ones who would stand in the gap for the nation to avoid destruction. Because He found none, the nation came under judgement. (Ezekiel 22:30)

Friends of God have a voice with God and access to His favour. You can rest assured that not only do you have favour, but God listens to you when you plead the case of someone else. We must live with the consciousness of divine favour resting on our lives. The Scriptures say in Isaiah 8:12, not to fear what they fear. Intercede for your friends and family, even those who are unbelieving and perhaps wicked. Intercede for the lost and trust that God will hear you and heed.

6. According to 1 Peter 2:9 believers are a chosen people and God's special possession. Do you think this implies favour and influence with God?

_____

_____

_____

_____

_____

7. How did Lot's later actions show that he did not have the confidence of a friend of God?

8. What would you say to a person who feels that they are too sinful to find favour with God?

9. List areas in your life where you need to apply this revelation that you have favour and influence with God. Include relevant scriptures to meditate on.

10. Think of the people you relate to at home, at work and in church. Let the Holy Spirit show you areas in which your intercession can make a difference in their lives. List them.

Intercessory prayer is a powerful act whereby a person who has influence with God asks for favour on behalf of another who is in difficulty.

Prayer

1. Pray that the challenging circumstances other people face will touch you deeply.

2. Pray for the heart of an intercessor.

3. Pray that the favour on your life will spill over towards your entourage.

4. Pray for one person who needs divine intervention swiftly in their lives.

Prophetic Declarations

1. Declare that you are today, tomorrow and forever a true friend of God. Celebrate it.

2. Declare that you are highly favoured of God and precious to Him.

3. Declare that you are, like Abraham, an intercessor standing before God to avert disaster in people's lives.

4. Declare that those close to you will be spared evil because you have favour with God.

Your Prayer/Praise Points

-
-
-
-
-
-

Your Notes

This is where you write everything on your heart that does not fit into any of the other categories.

Your Decisions

Write out at least three things you have decided to do following this study.

4

THE FAITHFULNESS OF GOD - DIVINE INTERVENTION

Is anything too hard for the Lord? (Genesis. 18:14).

THIS SCRIPTURE IS A BLANKET STATEMENT OF divine possibilities that every believer must appropriate. When we believe it, we learn to rest. And rest we should, despite the challenges of human existence. Abraham the friend of God lived in a world of labour and conflict. He faced personal challenges, made mistakes and yet, God continually intervened to help him. God keeps His promises. He intervenes when everything seems to be contrary to His promise. At an age when her contemporaries were looking to the grave, Sarah became a mother.

Without the faithfulness of God and His intervention, the story of Abraham would have ended in Egypt, where he fled for food and allowed Pharaoh to take his wife. Isaac would never have been born and the plan of God for a new nation to come from Abraham's loins would have been aborted. The plan of God for redemption would have been stalled until God found another man. But He intervened repeatedly in Abraham's life to put him back on course and fulfil His promises. One of the great reasons for security that a believer has is the faithfulness of God.

Scripture

Read Genesis. 17. Write a summary of the chapter.

Questions

Read the chapter in the book to answer the following questions.

1. How would you describe faithfulness as a divine attribute?

2. What is the condition for enjoying the faithfulness of God in full measure and why?

3. What is your understanding of divine intervention from the passages quoted in the book? Does it happen? If so when?

4. Some people say everything we have is based on our merit. Does the life of Abraham validate this? Explain your perspective.

5. How is the faithfulness of God demonstrated in Genesis 17:19-22?

INSIGHT

THE KINDNESS OF GOD

Then he prayed, Lord, God of my master Abraham, make me successful today, and show kindness to my master Abraham (Genesis 24:12).

Is anything too hard for the Lord? When we understand that God intervenes on behalf of His friends, we lose all penchant for worry and insomnia. Jesus made it clear that all our worrying could not make the slightest difference to our wellbeing, who indeed can add a cubit to his life? We can trust Him in every circumstance. When Abraham's servant was sent to find a wife for his master's son, he knew who to turn to. The servant who had lived with Abraham for so many years knew that his master had a God who was faithful. He prayed to the God of His master and God answered him. He intervened to give a wife to Isaac. And when Isaac saw Rebekah, he loved her. God chose well.

Many marital woes and errors would be avoided if we would look to His faithfulness in these matters and do so early. Marriage is precious in the sight of God and any believer who wants to fulfil their destiny must be very careful who they marry. Imagine if Abraham's servant had brought home a wicked young woman who made life hell for Isaac. How much grief that would have caused Abraham! But our God is faithful to give guidance and orchestrate divine encounters.

When with age we acquire greater wisdom, we sometimes look back on our lives and wonder at some wrong decisions we took. But even more surprising is how God intervened to bail us out. King David, in his later years, was compelled to testify that he had never seen God abandon either the righteous or their offspring. And unsurprisingly so, after all, anyone would have thought after David committed adultery with Bathsheba, that it would be over for him forever. Rather, after his punishment, he experienced astonishing divine faithfulness despite his unfaithfulness.

6. What do you think God did specifically to answer the prayer of Abraham's servant and how does it show faithfulness and kindness?

_____
_____
_____
_____
_____

7. Think of the stories of people you know who have experienced divine intervention in the area of marriage. What lessons do you draw from their experience with God?

_____
_____
_____
_____
_____

8. Enumerate specific situations of divine intervention in any area of your life. What did those situations teach you about God?

_____
_____
_____
_____

9. What do we learn from Genesis 25:7-11 about the faithfulness of God?

10. One of the wonderful things about being in good relationship with God is the certainty of His presence. Do you agree, as the book says, that "a person who is walking in divine friendship needs to buy himself a very good pillow,"?

Prayer

1. Pray and thank God for His incomparable faithfulness and continuous intervention in your life.

2. Pray for a revelation of His faithfulness and kindness so that you will always expect good from Him. Pray to be free of all fear about your life and your future.

3. Break the power of fear and anxiety over your life.

4. Pray that, like Abraham, your life will testify of His faithfulness and show that He has blessed you in all things.

Prophetic Declarations

1. Declare that as a friend of God, you enjoy the faithfulness of God daily.

2. Declare that you are not alone, nor are you misunderstood or abandoned.

3. Declare that every challenge in your life has a good and enduring solution in God.

4. Declare your confidence that everywhere and in all things, God intervenes on your behalf and you always have victory.

Your Prayer/Praise Points

-
-
-
-
-

Your Notes

This is where you write everything on your heart that does not fit into any of the other categories.

Your Decisions

Write out at least three things you have decided to do following this study.

BOOK TWO - BECOMING A FRIEND OF GOD

WHAT ARE THE CHARACTERISTICS OF A FRIEND of God? How do we become friends of God? We know that in Christ we have been positioned in divine friendship, however, many do not experience the reality of it.

We want to further explore the Word of God and observe those who walked closely with God like Enoch, Moses and of course Abraham. Let us see what truths we can glean from them. What do we do, how do we live to enter into full enjoyment of divine friendship?

> We have no more pressing need than to attune our hearts to God and become men and women He can boast about.

2.1

KNOW HIM

But more than that, I count everything as loss compared to the priceless privilege and supreme advantage of knowing Christ Jesus my Lord [and of growing more deeply and thoroughly acquainted with Him—a joy unequaled]. For His sake I have lost everything, and I consider it all garbage, so that I may gain Christ (Philippians 3:8 (AMP)).

IT IS QUITE COMMON TO HEAR PEOPLE say they do not believe in God. And when you ask them why they say so, they give you passionate arguments that reflect a total lack of understanding of who God is. 'Well, I cannot believe in a God who does or who is...', and they make some preposterous assertion about God. And you think, 'who is that'? Conversely, there are others who do say they believe in God, who happily describe their understanding of 'God' and the relationship they claim to have with 'Him'. And you realise that they must be referring to some divinity other than the God of the Bible. They do not know Him.

Unfortunately, neither do many believers. He remains distant, inscrutable, might I dare say, for some, irascible. God wants to be known. He has promised that those who seek Him will find Him. By faith we receive our salvation, by knowing Him deeply, we grow in relationship and intimacy. Our quest for greater understanding of God and His ways must be unceasing.

Ignorance of the other is an enemy of intimacy. And that ignorance is visible when we try to tell people about Him. Sharing a few stock phrases we have picked up is just not good enough. His identity must be real to us. Not only must it be real to us, but we must also affirm it despite the opposition of our generation. Moses understood this; though reticent, he was wise. As explored in the chapter, despite the astounding encounter at the burning bush, he still was wise enough to ask for God's identity. 'When they ask me for your name, what should I tell them', he asked?

SCRIPTURE

Read Acts 7:2-4; Exodus 3:13-15. Write a summary of the two passages.

QUESTIONS

Read the chapter in the book to answer the following questions.

1. What are the four dimensions of knowing God identified in the chapter?

___

2. Why did Moses ask for God's identity, and why is it important?

___

3. What difference did knowing the identity of Jesus make to the life of the Apostle Paul?

4. Read the following quote in context and explain it: "we are in grave danger of adopting the god of the 'Canaanites' and making a golden calf whom we call 'Elohim'". What do you think?

5. Does Acts 7:2-4 show that Abraham knew God? Explain your position.

Insight

KNOW HIS CHARACTER

The attributes of God declare the character of God. It is worth taking time to meditate on them. What is God like? Beyond the first encounter, there must be ongoing progress in revelation. The apostle Paul encountered Jesus on the road to Damascus, and he was so captivated by Jesus and His truth that he gave up everything for Him. And yet he still wanted more intimacy. His cry was to know the Lord. And his entire life was one of increasing revelation.

True friendship requires intimacy and is predicated on trust. This means that we must know the nature and the character of God and be convinced of His goodness. The goodness, kindness, love, mercy of God must be real to us before we can truly walk with Him.

Knowing God's expectations and going along with them is also essential for true friendship. In the book, I discuss how many believers agonise endlessly over the choices they need to make. They receive simple directions from God and cannot bring themselves to obey. For many, convenience is often the barometer for judging the validity of divine direction. We must be convinced of His faithfulness.

> For many, convenience is often the barometer for judging the validity of divine direction.

6. List 5 ways described in the book in which knowing the character of God enhances our friendship with Him.

_____
_____
_____
_____
_____
_____
_____

7. What is your response to this quote from the book? "Have you ever felt that deep in your heart you were slightly suspicious of God's intentions?" What difference has reading the book made?

_____
_____
_____
_____
_____
_____
_____

8. What is the connection drawn in the book between knowing God's character and giving?

_____
_____
_____
_____
_____

9. What is the connection between knowing what God wants and becoming friends of God?

10. How do we know God? List at least four points given in the book and comment on them.

PRAYER

1. Pray that you will know God—His identity, His character, His purposes, and all He desires you to know.

2. Pray that every wrong imagination and every misconception about Him be wiped away from your mind.

3. Pray that you will be sensitive to His heart and to His desires.

4. Pray that you will love Him as fully and wholly as He wants you to love Him.

PROPHETIC DECLARATIONS

1. Declare that you are a lover of God, that you have no greater desire than to please Him.

2. Declare you know what God wants and you want what God wants.

3. Declare that you will honour Him every day of your life.

4. Declare that you will live in symbiosis with God all your life.

YOUR PRAYER/PRAISE POINTS

-
-
-
-
-
-
-

Your Notes

This is where you write everything on your heart that does not fit into any of the other categories.

Your Decisions

Write out at least three things you have decided to do following this study.

2.2

TRUST HIM

> And the scripture was fulfilled that says, "Abraham believed God, and it was credited to him as righteousness," and he was called God's friend (James 2:23).

TRUST IS ESSENTIAL TO FRIENDSHIP. NO TRUE relationship can subsist and thrive in an atmosphere of suspicion and recriminations. If we are to be true friends of God, we must grow in faith. It is fashionable in some circles to celebrate doubt as though there was some virtue in disbelieving the truths of the faith or in questioning the character of God.

Quite the contrary, the Scriptures affirm the need for steadfast faith in all circumstances. In so doing we honour the Lord and enjoy the benefits He freely grants the believer. Abraham had some low points in his life, but he matured and grew in faith. And the final testimony of his life was that he believed God, and he was called God's friend.

The obvious inference is that those who do not believe God cannot be called His friends. In fact, those who do not believe Him endanger their lives and their destinies. Such was the case of the generation of Israelites who perished in the wilderness instead of inheriting the Promised Land.

And such was the case of King Saul who did not trust God but rather feared the people. He lost the favour of God and had a wretched end.

SCRIPTURE

Read Genesis 18:18-19. Explain the concept in this passage.

QUESTIONS

Read the chapter in the book to answer the following questions.

1. Why was Abraham's trust in God so essential for their friendship?

2. Review the discussion in the chapter about God's willingness to trust a human being.

3. What is the proof cited in the chapter that God trusted Abraham? Explain.

4. Read the passage in the book on the people who died in the wilderness. Then read Numbers 14:11. Comment extensively on the text and the Scripture.

_____

5. What does it mean to trust God? List and comment on the three points given in the text.

_____

INSIGHT

TRUST OR DISTRUST?

To trust God is to have confidence in Him, in His goodness and love. It is to believe He has the power to act in conformity with the dictates of His goodness and love. We believe not only that God is good, but that He has the power to, and will do good. So we do not shy away from Him or distrust Him, rather we are eager to hear and do what He wants.

Unfortunately, there are many who are not experiencing this. In the chapter we look at seven reasons why people have difficulty trusting God. Too often we treat His commands with trepidation and suspicion unless He spells out in black and white exactly how things will turn out. And even then, we ask for a sign. We fear He will invoke His sovereignty and leave us out in the cold.

Many believers, though few will admit it, almost treat God's instructions as irrational interruptions into their ordered, well thought out existence. And when they do obey, it is as one humouring an irascible deity. They go along with Him despite His 'unorthodox ways'.

We can and should learn to trust God. The chapter focuses on five ways to grow in faith in God. It is possible to fear God and yet love Him, be comfortable with Him and happy in Him.

6. How do you reconcile divine sovereignty and trust in God for a particular outcome?

> Many believers, though few will admit it, almost treat God's instructions as irrational interruptions into their ordered, well thought out existence.

7. List the seven reasons given for our difficulty in trusting God. Relate these to your own experience.

8. Comment on this statement "People are unconsciously programmed to expect the worst to cushion themselves from the potential impact of non-fulfilment."

9. What are the five ways given to develop our trust in God? Apply them to your own life.

10. Explain the 'kill the bear' reference in the passage. What is your opinion of this? Is there a 'bear' in your life right now and how will you handle it?

Prayer

1. Pray for a revelation of God, that you will know Him and trust Him.

2. Repent of past distrust of God, renouncing disappointment at delay where it has sapped your confidence in God.

3. Commit to walk in faith and consider Him faithful.

4. Pray against demonic attacks on your mind, declaring the faithfulness of God.

Prophetic Declarations

1. Declare that you are a child of light and that you walk in revelation and insight.

2. Declare that you are a man or woman of faith, that you trust God implicitly in all things.

3. Declare that you believe in His goodness and power to manifest His goodness in you and through you.

4. Declare that you stand firmly against all demonic assaults against your faith and you always believe the truth about God.

Your Prayer/Praise Points

-
-
-
-
-
-

Your Notes

This is where you write everything on your heart that does not fit into any of the other categories.

Your Decisions

Write out at least three things you have decided to do following this study.

2.3

AGREE WITH HIM

Can two walk together, except they be agreed? (Amos 3:3).

I RECEIVE FREQUENT REQUESTS FOR PRAYER FROM WOMEN who are going through challenges in their marriages because of a lack of harmony. They just cannot seem to see eye to eye about most things with their spouses. There are frequent misunderstandings that degenerate into discord and hostility. Often, these women give in, but then live with resentment in their hearts against their spouse. Sometimes it is parents with their children. They cannot seem to have a simple conversation without irritation and rancour. When that happens, intimacy becomes impossible.

In the book, I tell the story of a friendship that started out very badly but eventually became one of the closest friendships I have had in my life. And that was because God intervened. There is hope. But what happens when the disagreement is in our relationship with God? The Fall came about because man disrupted the harmony with God and the outcome was devastating. All agreement and concord evaporated.

Adam and his wife hid from God. His vision of them was now different from their vision of themselves. The agreement was lost, they had to leave. Separation had come. Man could no longer walk in intimacy with God. They had "lost sensitivity to divine ways" and their thinking became perverted. It became distorted, alien to divine logic.

Scripture

Read Isaiah 55:1-9. Note the main points in this passage.

Questions

Read the chapter in the book to answer the following questions.

1. Define harmony. Paint a picture of a harmonious relationship with God.

2. Is worship an accurate demonstration of harmony with God? Explain.

3. "We demonstrate our agreement and harmony with God when we are faced with a challenge or an instruction—when something is required of us, not when something is given to us". What is your view of this statement from the chapter?

4. List five or more of the reasons given in the book why humans have difficulty agreeing with God. What is your perspective?

5. List some ways in which Abraham's life showed his agreement with God.

INSIGHT

ELEVATION THROUGH AGREEMENT

God is inviting us to lead an extraordinary life. He took Abraham out of the ordinary, and by agreeing with God, Abraham's life became wonderful beyond his wildest imaginings. Everyone who has walked in agreement with God has seen God elevate his thinking, desires, imagination and plans. And each one has lived a life greater than they could have envisaged.

Bishop David Oyedepo, a well-known Nigerian minister, leads one of the largest congregations in the world and founded what is today one of the best universities globally. That is remarkable in itself, but even more so given the location. All this happened in a location miles from civilisation and totally contrary to all principles of church growth or development.

When they went to view the land, they travelled so far out of town that he had no thought of ever taking the ministry there. By the time they arrived, he had made up his mind that the distance was too great. Yet, as they knelt to pray, he was startled to hear the voice of God tell him 'this is the place'.

The location was the haven of occultic powers, witches, wizards and all manner of diabolical entities. He went into the lion's den on God's instructions and Jesus took over. The ministry moved to another level, the church exploded in growth in the middle of nowhere. They built a 50,000 seater sanctuary in one year, debt free and without begging for money. He had the choice, agree or disagree. He agreed, and the rest is history. Over 100,000 worshippers gather there every week. Their agreement with God was their elevation.

6. How does the life of Jesus demonstrate agreement with the Father?

7. Some claim that they may agree that God's way is good, however, they are under no obligation to do things His way because they are only human. What is wrong with this perspective?

8. How do we bring ourselves to agree with God?

9. Read Romans 12.2. How will you apply this to your life?

10. Give examples of people in the Bible and in your entourage who walked in agreement with God and say how it affected their lives.

Prayer

1. Pray against every hostility and discord that you might entertain in your relationship with God.

2. Pray against resentment and possible disappointments in your heart towards the Lord.

3. Pray a prayer of submission and agreement with the will of God in all its ramifications.

4. Pray a prayer of acknowledgement that God's ways are perfect, ask for a willing heart to always agree with Him.

Prophetic Declarations

1. Declare that you renounce every ill feeling and discord in your heart towards the Lord.

2. Declare that you fully yield to the Holy Spirit in all things.

3. Declare that you are a child of God, consequently, you have the mind of Christ.

4. Declare that you are and will be in harmony with God all the days of your life.

Your Prayer/Praise Points

-
-
-
-
-
-

YOUR NOTES

This is where you write everything on your heart that does not fit into any of the other categories.

Your Decisions

Write out at least three things you have decided to do following this study.

2.4

OBEY HIM

You are my friends if you do what I command you (John 15:14).

WE HAVE SEEN THAT TWO CANNOT WALK together unless they are in agreement. And from the above Scripture, we learn that we cannot walk in friendship with God if we do not obey Him. Genesis 12:4 says that Abraham went 'as the Lord had told him'. In other words, he obeyed. No wonder, God called him His friend.

Friendship by its very nature is reciprocal. Non-believers may wonder what use it is to them to know God. However, as Christians, we need no convincing that it is very much to our advantage to be a friend of God. The question is, what accrues to God from our friendship? Beyond the satisfaction of His heart of love, my obedience and cooperation will serve to further His purposes. But am I living in such a way that He can consider me a friend? Am I doing what He commands?

True friends are those through whom He establishes and prospers His purposes in the world.

Consider Noah. His testimony is that he did everything 'just as the Lord had commanded him'. What use would have been the astounding promise of deliverance from the flood had Noah been unwilling to build the Ark? We can get excited when the Lord makes huge promises to us, but we must factor in the obedience component. And that is when we please the Lord. True friends are those through whom He establishes and prospers His purposes in the world.

Each one of us in our sphere of activity can be a true friend of God by obeying Him and working for His purposes. Bishop Oyedepo obeyed and left the vibrant metropolis of Lagos for a forest where occultic activity held sway. In so doing, he yielded to divine purpose, and God's desire to raise a mighty work was furthered by his obedience.

> True friends are those through whom He establishes and prospers His purposes in the world.

Scripture

Read Genesis 22:10-18. What is the primary lesson of this passage?

QUESTIONS

Read the chapter in the book to answer the following questions.

1. Define obedience.

2. Give 5 ways in which Abraham demonstrated obedience.

3. What is God's reaction to Abraham's obedience as told in Genesis 22.16-18?

4. Discuss how Noah demonstrated obedience. What can we learn from God's reaction to his obedience?

_____
_____
_____
_____
_____
_____
_____

5. Explain how Jesus showed obedience. What can we learn from the Father's response to His obedience?

_____
_____
_____
_____
_____
_____
_____
_____
_____
_____
_____

INSIGHT

LOVE AND OBEDIENCE

In John 14:21-24, Jesus shows the connection between loving Him and obeying Him. It is a striking passage. He says that those who love Him will obey Him. And He and the Father will come and dwell in them. In other words, they will now have intimacy with God. Let us not sweep obedience under the carpet. No one can claim to love Jesus who refuses to obey Him. He makes the point that His Words are not just His own but those of the Father. Keeping His commandments is proof of love. And the outcome is friendship and intimacy.

Conversely, those who do not obey Him demonstrate their lack of love for Him. Consequently, we can deduce, they forfeit His offer of intimacy. Clearly, the price of disobedience is much too high. It is much higher than punishment, sickness, demonic attacks or any of the other things that people fear. It is a loss of intimacy with God and revelation of God; a most terrible price to pay.

> The price of disobedience is much too high.

6. Does obedience still matter under the New Covenant? Why?

_____
_____
_____
_____
_____
_____
_____

7. Why do people disobey God? List at least four of the reasons given in the chapter. Add more of your own.

8. "Disobedience is a robber". How would you respond to this quote from the book?

9. In what way have you demonstrated obedience? What do you expect from God?

10. With the help of the Holy Spirit, meditate on areas where you need to work on your obedience. Note instructions you had previously neglected and now intend to execute.

Prayer

1. Pray and repent of disobedience.

2. Pray to be be delivered from all carelessness about obeying God; and that all you have lost through disobedience be restored.

3. Pray that you will grow in courage and faith to obey instinctively, irrespective of the cost.

4. Pray that you will clearly understand what God wants you to do in every situation.

5. Pray that God will surround you with people who are passionate about obeying God.

Prophetic Declarations

1. Declare that you are an obedient child of God.

2. Declare that you love the teachings of Jesus and all the ways of God.

3. Declare that you are sensitive to, and follow God's direction.

4. Declare that you receive wisdom and strength to do all that God requires of you.

Your Prayer/Praise Points

-
-
-
-
-

YOUR NOTES

This is where you write everything on your heart that does not fit into any of the other categories.

YOUR DECISIONS

Write out at least three things you have decided to do following this study.

2.5

COMMUNE WITH HIM

> God is faithful, who has called you into fellowship with his Son, Jesus Christ our Lord (1 Corinthians 1:9).

COMMUNION CAN BE DEFINED AS INTIMATE FELLOWSHIP, intimate communication, sharing of emotions, feelings, close companionship. This is the privilege we enjoy in Christ. Once enemies of God, we have been brought into divine friendship. And we are called to fellowship. Communion with God is a defining characteristic of any friend of God and is also essential to becoming a friend of God. God desires us to be intimate, to be close to Him; not just 'good' Christians.

Several Old Testament saints, in their pursuit of fellowship with God, deprive us of all excuse to do otherwise. Abraham pursued communion with God in diverse ways as seen in the chapter. Others like Enoch were exemplary in their walk with God. While some men were plunging deeper into wickedness, Enoch was communing with and serving God. He embodied three necessary dimensions of any man, faith in God, fellowship with God and eternity with God.

The Bible tells us very little about Enoch. We know that he was married, bore children, walked with God and God took him. His extraordinary testimony is proof that none is doomed to inherit the spiritual weaknesses of their entourage. We can be exemplary in our intimacy with the Father despite the surrounding scepticism.

SCRIPTURE

Read Ephesians. 5:1-14. Write a summary of the passage.

QUESTIONS

Read the chapter in the book and answer the following questions.

1. What is communion with God?

2. How did Abraham fellowship with God?

3. The chapter discusses the remarkable story of Enoch. What lessons have you learnt from his life??

4. How did Noah and Moses exemplify communion with God?

5. 'Living like the Master' discusses how we have been brought near. What implication does this have for friendship with God?

INSIGHT

JESUS OUR EXAMPLE

In Jesus, we see how a human being can live in fellowship with God. Jesus often went away alone to be in communion with the Father. He went to lonely places, fled the crowds, and stayed up all night. Jesus showed us how desirable fellowship with God can be. Our Lord lived in symbiosis with the Father and the Holy Spirit. He said in John 14:11:

'I am in the Father and the Father is in me'.

His life exemplified the power of intimacy, the beauty of sharing the thoughts of God. He lived such that He knew what God was saying and doing. And He did and said the same. That is huge!

What God wants is a people who think like Him, who see as He sees and who act as He acts. Our Lord was a perfect embodiment of that. And it must be our ambition, quest and pursuit.

We can all be more like God than we are right now. The key is to desire and pursue it. However, too often we pursue emotional and material needs instead of spiritual intimacy with God.

> What God wants is a people who think like Him, who see as He sees and who act as He acts.

6. How did Jesus exemplify communion with the Father? Indicate some relevant Scriptures.

_____

_____

_____

_____

7. List and explain the five points given to grow in fellowship with God.

8. Explain the concept of 'walking in darkness' as developed in the chapter.

9. Describe the outcome of communion with God, what the book calls 'a beautiful existence'.

10. Give a general assessment of your communion with God. What are the improvements you need to make?

Prayer

1. Pray for hunger for divine fellowship.

2. Pray for supernatural revelation in the Word of God that will cause you to be captivated by God.

3. Pray that you will see God as He is.

4. Pray for a passion to walk in the light.

Prophetic Declarations

1. Declare that you are a child of light and not of darkness.

2. Declare that you are passionate about the Person and presence of God.

3. Declare that you yield your entire life to God and defer to Him in all things.

4. Declare that you are sensitive to the needs of the kingdom and know the heart of God.

Your Prayer/Praise Points

-
-
-
-
-
-
-

Your Notes

This is where you write everything on your heart that does not fit into any of the other categories.

Your Decisions

Write out at least three things you have decided to do following this study.

2.6

Honour Him

> How long will this wicked community grumble against me? I have heard the complaints of these grumbling Israelites (Numbers 14:27).

TO HONOUR GOD IS TO RECOGNISE HIS great worth, to esteem Him highly. It is to consider Him, and all that pertains to Him weighty, of extreme importance, and to treat them with the utmost respect.

The prophet Malachi was seriously upset with the people of his day who were self-absorbed and self-focused while neglecting the house of God. They did not honour God with their finances. We see a lot of that today as well. Many believers ask God for diverse blessings and are very demanding towards the church. They require total care for every area of their spiritual lives while being thoroughly negligent towards the work of God.

They do not give, they squabble about tithing and they are not available to serve. Their lives are hugely important to them but the affairs of the kingdom scarcely so. True friends of God will care about what God cares about. The Scriptures show us many other ways of honouring God as detailed in the chapter.

Integrity in our affairs honours God. Abraham made a remarkable statement to a foreign king that showed how much he honoured the Lord. Abraham had gone to rescue Lot who had been taken captive, caught in the crossfire in the war between several kings. When the victory was won, thanks to Abraham and his men, the king of Sodom offered for Abraham to keep the goods.

Rather than jump at the opportunity to enrich himself Abraham rejected the offer. He told the king of Sodom that he had sworn an oath to the Lord His God. He would not accept anything belonging to him, not even a thread or the strap of a sandal. That way, the king of Sodom would never be able to say that it was thanks to him that Abraham became rich.

Abraham did not run after the goods, his focus was on honouring the Lord. He had respect for God's reputation and that affected his choices and decisions. He honoured God with his integrity. And when he encountered the priest of God, he gave him his tithe.

SCRIPTURE

Read Malachi 3:13-18. Write a summary of the passage.

QUESTIONS

Read the chapter in the book and answer the following questions.

1. Explain the connection between honour and gratitude.

2. What are the different ways in which we may honour the Lord?

3. What do you think of Malachi's contention with the people of his day and how do you relate that to the church today?

4. How did Abraham honour God with his finances?

5. How else did Abraham honour God? Give examples.

INSIGHT

A GRATEFUL ATTITUDE

In the chapter, we examine different ways in which we show honour to God. The first passage deals with an instance where the people rejected God's plan, complained about their leaders and wanted to set in motion an alternative plan. They dishonoured God because they grumbled against Him. They showed their lack of confidence in God. They did not think Him trustworthy.

The plan of God is perfect, but its fulfilment involves challenges for us. That is what the people of Israel did not understand, and hardship turned them against God. An all too common attitude, unfortunately. Many believers can identify with that even though we often prefer to look down our noses at the 'fickle' Israelites.

When tough times come, many resort to complaining. They suffer acute memory loss concerning the goodness of God towards them. They are testifying one week and moaning the next.

We must honour the Lord with a grateful attitude, thanking, praising and worshipping Him continually.

> When tough times come, many resort to complaining. They suffer acute memory loss concerning the goodness of God towards them.

6. What does the chapter say about honouring God with our worship?

7. What do we learn from the book about how the Holy Spirit helps us to honour God? What is your perspective?

8. Do you agree with the statement in the chapter that we honour God with our service? How and why?

9. Read Psalm 78:19-22. Comment on what they did to dishonour God.

10. Think about your own life. Write down ways in which you feel you have honoured God and ways in which you have not.

Prayer

1. Pray to express your gratitude to God for all His goodness.
2. Pray for personal integrity that honours God.
3. Pray that you will be useful to God.
4. Pray a prayer of total surrender to divine purpose.

Prophetic Declarations

1. Declare that you will honour the Lord all your life.
2. Declare your gratitude for all His goodness to you.
3. Declare your absolute faith in God and total dependence on Him.
4. Declare that you will honour the Lord with your finances.

Your Prayer Points

-
-
-
-
-
-
-
-
-

Your Notes

This is where you write everything on your heart that does not fit into any of the other categories.

Your Decisions

Write out at least three things you have decided to do following this study.

•

Epilogue

I PRAY THAT THIS SHORT STUDY AND THE book itself have spurred you on to greater hunger for God and deeper intimacy with Him. We were made by and for God; and to live is to live in Him. In Jesus we have been given full access to God; and we are as close to God as we have sought to be.

The psalmist exclaims in Psalm 8 'what is man?'. He is stunned that God whose splendour is displayed in the heavens, in the great lights, would stoop to even consider man and care for him. Not only that, He has crowned him with glory and honour, made him a little lower than God.

No pat theological explanations can do away with this astonishment and wonder. Even more wondrous is that God desires friendship with man. May we see the greatness of this privilege and respond with eagerness.

We pray you have been blessed by this book. Please take a moment to leave a review on one of the online sites. Your review will help increase the visibility of the book so more people can be blessed. You will be contributing to getting this message out.

Do not forget to sign up for the newsletter on www.bolaoged.com **and download your free eBook.**

About the Author

BOLA OGEDENGBE is a lover of God. She is an author, pastor and teacher. She is the founding pastor of ABBA HOUSE church in Paris, France and heads the prophetic ministry The Theophilus Company.

She is a former conference interpreter, speaks five languages and has travelled extensively globally. She has a heart for the nations and a passion to take the gospel to the world. Her weekly television programme Passion for God equips believers to live powerfully for God as she shares deep insights into God's Word.

She is a longstanding blogger and author of many books in English and French.

Other books by author

- An Amazing Life (Book)
- Reborn, A New Identity
- Reborn A New Identity (30 day Workbook)
- An Eye to the Crown
- Appelez à l'Existence (Call into existence)
- Le Feu de Dieu (The Fire of God)

Sign up on her blogs for updates and free ebooks
English blog : www.bolaoged.com
French blog : www.oliviaoged.com

BOLA OLIVIA OGEDENGBE

www.ingramcontent.com/pod-product-compliance
Lightning Source LLC
LaVergne TN
LVHW081451060526
838201LV00050BA/1762